Brass

Wendy Lynch

Heinemann Library
Chicago, Illinois

© 2002 Reed Educational & Professional Publishing
Published by Heinemann Library,
an imprint of Reed Educational & Professional Publishing,
Chicago, Illinois

Customer Service 888-454-2279

Visit our website at www.heinemannlibrary.com

Designed by Visual Image
Illustration by Jane Watkins
Originated by Dot Gradations
Printed and bound in South China

06 05 04 03 02
10 9 8 7 6 5 4 3 2 1

Library of Congress Cataloging-in-Publication Data
Lynch, Wendy, 1945-
    Brass / Wendy Lynch.
      p. cm. -- (Musical instruments)
    Includes bibliographical references (p.   ) and index.
    ISBN 1-58810-233-5
    1. Brass instruments--Juvenile literature. [1. Brass instruments.] I.
    Title. II. Series.
    ML933 .L96 2001
    788.9'19--dc21

                                    2001002882

Acknowledgments
The Publishers would like to thank the following for permission to reproduce photographs: pp. 4, 19, 23 Pictor; pp. 5, 26 Stone; pp. 6, 7, 10 Photodisc; p. 8 Richard Alton/Photofusion; p. 9 Ray Roberts/Photofusion; pp. 11, 15, 16 Odile Noel/Redfern; p. 12 The Stock Market; pp. 14, 20, 22, 24 Corbis; p. 17 Robert Harding; p. 18 Derek Allan/Travel Ink; p. 21 Zefa/Powerstock; p. 25 Rex; p. 27 Paul Massey/Redfern; pp. 28, 29 Gareth Boden.
Cover photograph reproduced with permission of Photodisc.
Special thanks to Susan Lerner and Jonathan Dickmann for their comments in the preparation of this book.
Every effort has been made to contact copyright holders of any material reproduced in this book. Any omissions will be rectified in subsequent printings if notice is given to the publisher.

Some words are shown in bold, **like this.** You can find out what they mean by looking in the glossary.

Contents

Making Music Together

There are many musical instruments in the world. Each instrument makes a different sound. We can make music together by playing these instruments in a band or an **orchestra.**

Bands and orchestras are made
up of different groups of instruments.
One of these groups is called brass.
You can see brass instruments in this
brass band.

What Are Brass Instruments?

Brass instruments are often made of brass, a strong metal that does not **rust.** These instruments can also be made of other metals. Some are even made of wood, horn, or shell.

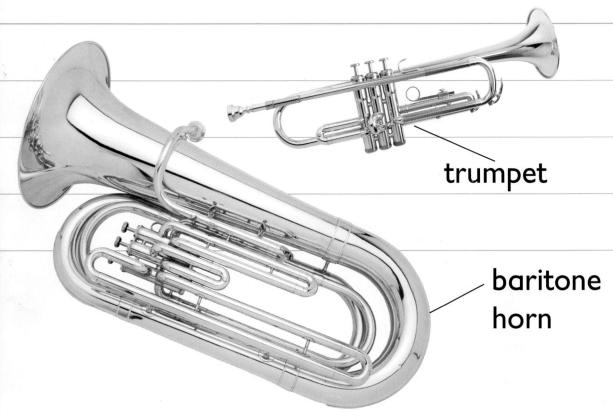

trumpet

baritone horn

To make a sound with a brass instrument, you press your lips against the **mouthpiece** and blow air into it. The **vibration** of your lips against the mouthpiece helps to make the sound.

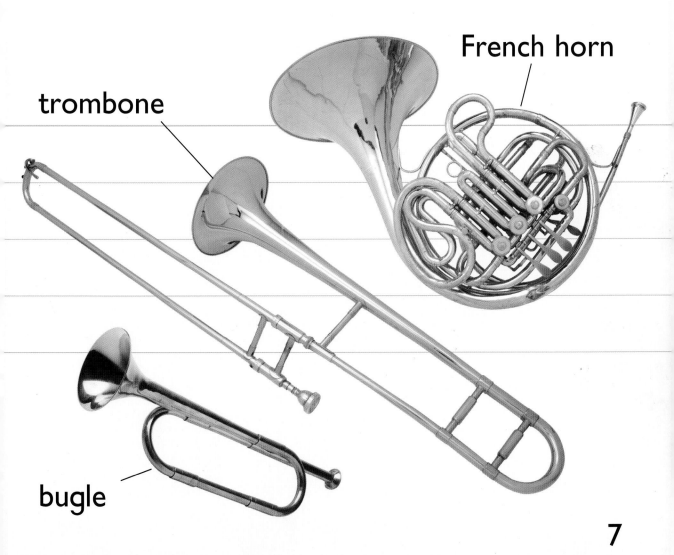

French horn

trombone

bugle

The Trumpet

The trumpet is one brass instrument that is often played in schools today. A teacher can show you how to play the trumpet. If you play alone, it is called playing **solo.**

You can also play the trumpet with other instruments in a small group, a brass band, or an **orchestra.**

Making a Sound

The trumpet is a long, thin, **coiled** metal tube. It has a **mouthpiece** at one end and a bell at the other. On top of the tube are three small buttons called **valves.**

bell

valves

mouthpiece

When you blow into the trumpet,
it makes air move quickly inside the
coiled tube. This movement is called
vibration. When the air vibrates, it
makes a sound.

Changing the Sound

To make a sound, you blow into the **mouthpiece.** Pressing the **valves** with your fingers makes the sound, or **pitch,** higher or lower. Changing the position of your lips can also change the sound.

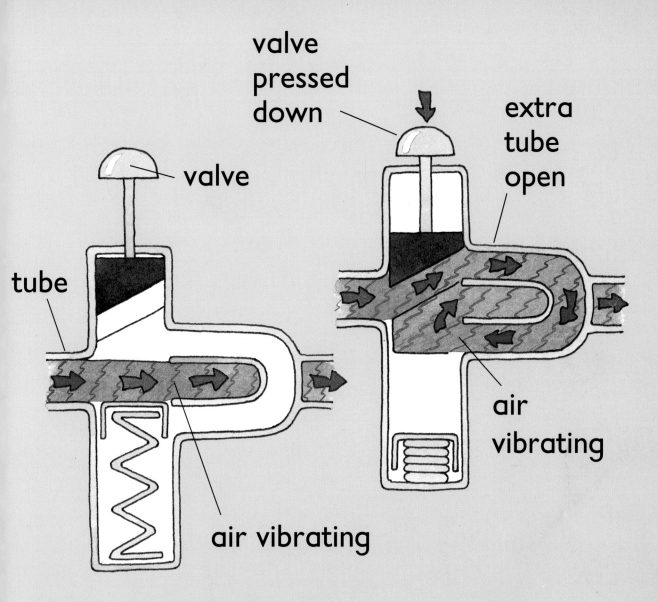

valve pressed down

valve

extra tube open

tube

air vibrating

air vibrating

If you press a valve, you open another part of the tube. The air inside has to go farther, so it **vibrates** more slowly, and the pitch gets lower.

The Cornet and the Trombone

The cornet is like a trumpet but smaller. You can sometimes hear the cornet playing **solo** in a brass band. It has a high, sweet sound. You can also hear the cornet in **jazz** music.

The trombone is played in a different way than other brass instruments. It has a long tube called a slide. You move the slide in and out to make the tube shorter or longer, changing the **pitch.**

Big Brass

The tuba is a large brass instrument with a rich, low sound. It takes a lot of breath to play the tuba because it is so big and the air has far to go. To play a tuba, you sit down with it on your knee.

The sousaphone is lighter than a tuba and is usually played standing up. The player stands inside the instrument's **coil.** He can even play while walking!

Marching Bands

In a marching band, you can hear brass and other instruments. All the players play their instruments while they move. They can read music from cards clipped onto the instruments.

Marching bands often lead parades on special days of celebration. Brass instruments have a strong sound that can be heard from a long way away.

The Wider Family

The bugle is a small horn without **valves** that can play only a few notes. Armies have used bugles for hundreds of years, usually to send signals to their soldiers.

The conch trumpet is made from a shell. It is a brass instrument because you play it in the same way, by pressing your lips against the **mouthpiece.** You can hear the sound from far away.

Around the World

You can find brass instruments all over the world. The dung chen comes from Tibet. You might hear this instrument in a **Buddhist temple.**

The didgeridoo comes from the branch of a tree in Australia. Insects eat the wood inside the branch until it is hollow. The **Aborigines** paint special designs on the wooden tube before they play it.

Famous Musicians and Composers

People have played the trumpet for hundreds of years. The **composer** Franz Joseph Haydn wrote a famous trumpet **concerto.**

You can also hear the cornet, trumpet, and trombone in **jazz** and **blues** music. Wynton Marsalis is well known for his expert trumpet playing.

Brass Music Today

Today, you can also hear brass instruments in **soul, rock,** and **pop** bands. The strong, clear sounds of brass instruments make them easy to hear, even when they play in a group.

A **synthesizer** is a keyboard that can **imitate** many different sounds. You can play the sounds of all the brass instruments using a synthesizer.

Sound Activities

You can feel what it is like to play a brass instrument. Close your lips together tightly. Now blow against your fingers until you make a noise. Can you feel your lips **vibrating?**

Roll a sheet of paper into a cone shape. Buzz your lips into the small end. You can change the sound by placing your hand against the large end as you blow. Try using a smaller cone. Does it make a different sound?

Thinking about Brass

You can find the answers to all of these questions in this book.

1. Why is brass good for making musical instruments?

2. What does a **valve** on a brass instrument do?

3. How is playing a trombone different from playing most other kinds of brass instruments?

4. Which brass instrument do you need to stand inside to play?

5. Where can you hear a dung chen?

Glossary

Aborigine one of the first people to live in Australia

blues style of music that is usually slow and sad

Buddhist belonging to the religion founded by Buddha

coiled curled or wound into a ring or loop

composer person who writes music

concerto piece of music, often for one instrument and an orchestra

imitate to copy

jazz style of music that is often made up as it is played

mouthpiece part of an instrument placed in or near the mouth

orchestra large group of musicians who play their instruments together

pitch highness or lowness of a sound or musical note

pop popular music

rock kind of pop music with a strong beat

rust to become covered with rust, a brown or red coating that forms on some metals

solo song or piece of music for one person

soul kind of pop music that is full of feeling

synthesizer electronic instrument that can make many different sounds

temple building for religious worship

valve moving part of an instrument that can change the path of air inside

vibrate to move back and forth very quickly

31

More Books to Read

Harris, Pamela K. *Trumpets.* Chanhassen, Minn.: The Child's World, Incorporated, 2000.

Kalman, Bobbie. *Musical Instruments from A to Z.* New York: Crabtree Publishing Company, 1997.

Turner, Barrie Carson. *Modern Instruments.* North Mankato, Minn.: Smart Apple Media, 2000.

Index